I0441091

GRACIOUSNESS ON THE GRIDIRON

Armor Fiction

ISBN: 978-1-096-59226-6

1st Edition
Paperback Print

Published By:
Armor Fiction Publishing Company
930 Dolley Madison Blvd.
McLean, VA 22101

Also By Rob Williams

Storm Cloud Rising (Author)

with Rob Williams (contributing)

Afghan's Lipstick Warriors: First Chronicle

Afghan's Lipstick Warriors: Darkness Falls

Printed in the United States of America

The educational institutions, teams, and characters depicted in this story are entirely fictitious. Any similarity to persons living or dead is merely coincidental.

DEDICATIONS

First and foremost a profound thank you to GOD. Every day is a blessing just to wake up, let alone be given the opportunity to live the life I do. I have seen the world, done many of the things I set out to do since my childhood, and continue to live a blessed life. Without my faith, and of course my family & friends, my success would not be what it is. Thank you for your help and support. I love you all!

To all of you who strap on a helmet, run those sprints, do that extra rep in the weight room, and take a second to appreciate the smells, sights, and sounds of game day, I thank you. I thank you for continuing to play the greatest game ever created. A game that exemplifies brotherhood, demands commitment, teaches humility and requires guts. Whether you play in front of a few hundred on Friday nights, a few thousand on Saturday afternoons, or tens of thousands on Sundays, the competitive nature of a football player is exactly the same, so keep it up!

TABLE OF CONTENTS

SMALL STAGE, BIG DREAMS

Division III college football and its players don't get much recognition. These young men will never experience a full ride scholarship, they will never see weekly coverage on major television networks, and most won't be sought after by NFL scouts. While a school like Penn State plays in front of 100,000 fans and millions watching on T.V., a DIII school might fill its stands with 2000 fans and, if they're lucky, have their game shown on a local television network adding another thousand to the viewing audience.

Instead, these athletes concentrate on their education and a career path for life ahead, but the love of football remains in their blood. Regardless of what others think about this level of play, Saturday afternoons are what these guys live for during the school year.

The lack of exposure doesn't mean Division III football is without its newsworthy events. Some of these guys do in fact get drafted to play in the NFL. Others brake national records and are mentioned from time to time by various sports networks. The National Championship game is now aired on ESPN allowing the entire country to see college football in its purest form.

With all this said, what occurred in 2006 on a cold fall day in Pennsylvania put Division III football and two of its schools in the national spotlight and forever into millions of hearts.

EVERYTHING CHANGES

It was a sunny, but cold fall Saturday afternoon in Northeastern Pennsylvania. The McKnight College stadium was filling up quickly, while two football teams were in the locker room discussing strategy and mentally preparing themselves for their biggest game of the year thus far. This was the semi-final round of the NCAA Division III football playoffs and the winner of this game would go on to play for a National Title. The McKnight College Spartans had been down this road before, making the playoffs a few times over the past ten years. On the other side of the gridiron was the Vernon College Titans and this was the school's first time ever reaching the playoffs.

As the fans settled into their seats, they were entertained by the home teams marching band. The crisp air was filled with the smell of hot dogs, hamburgers, and hot chocolate. The field was as green and beautifully decorated as a piece of art. Each side of the stadium bared witness to both team's school colors. You could see the majority of people wearing the McKnight gold and red, while Vernon fans contrasted with royal blue and white. The pride felt by those parents, friends, and classmates of the players couldn't be described with words, but it could be seen everywhere you looked. This was the embodiment of sport, it was damn near perfect, but one thing loomed dark on this day.

The McKnight College Spartans were dealing with a real life issue no school wants to face. Fellow college students, teammates, and especially parents are never prepared for situations like this, but they were dealing with the untimely passing of one of their own. Less than 24hrs before the start of this game, one of the Spartan's starting linebackers, Mike Albright, was tragically killed in a car accident only three miles from campus.

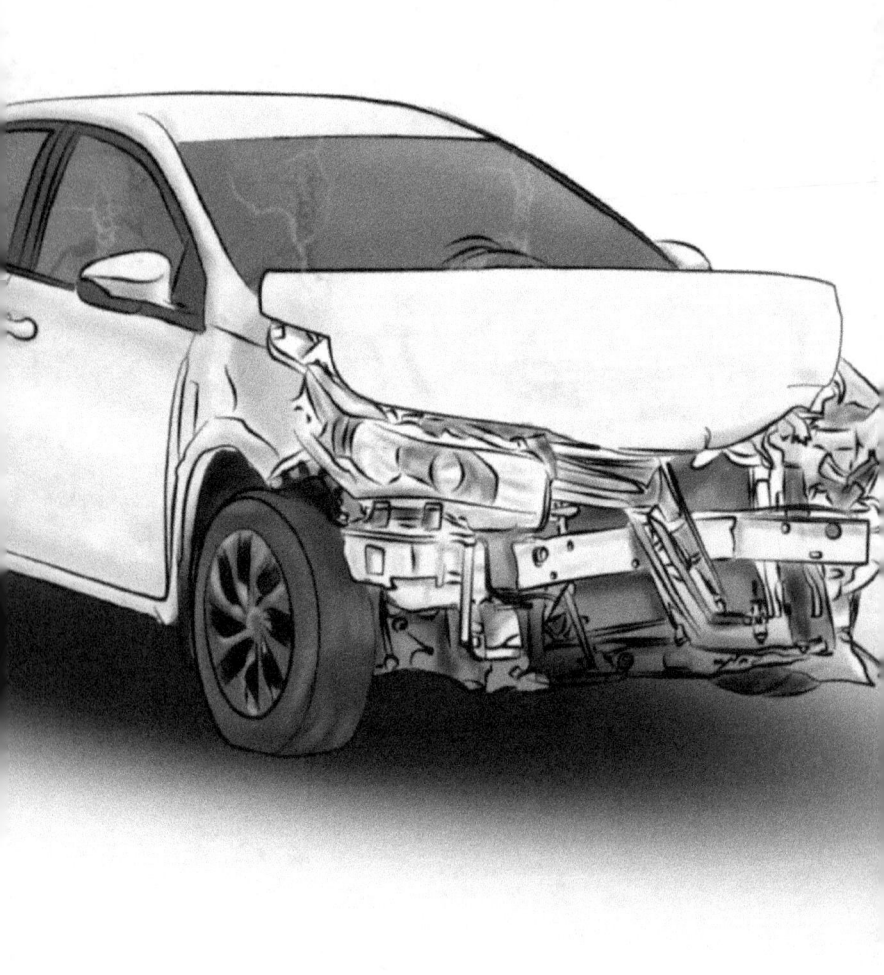

The Spartans coach, Joe Castle, received the call Friday afternoon around 1:30pm and knew he had to address the team immediately. He called an emergency meeting and had the players gather in the locker room. Once each player was accounted for, Coach Castle walked in and gazed upon his boys. They were innocent, youthful, excited, and eager to hear what their coach had to say. A few players noticed Mike wasn't there, but disregarded it figuring the coach already knew where he was. Little did they know the next five minutes would challenge their emotions and test their resolve as young men.

Coach Castle informed the boys of Mike's death. It wasn't easy, but he knew they needed to be told bluntly, as dancing around tragedy helps no one. The locker room fell silent, then filled with the weeping of young men. The shock was like a smack in the face. The reality of losing a friend and teammate now stood face to face with the boys. Coach Castle told them everything he knew. Mike was on his way back to campus and reports indicated someone lost control of their car and swerved into oncoming traffic. Mike tried to avoid the collision, but couldn't. He thought it was important for them to also hear that Mike passed immediately. As a young adult you don't always grasp the idea that someone you care for passing quickly is more comforting than them passing in pain.

As the players cried and hugged, trying to comfort each other and deal with news of losing one of their own, Coach Castle also knew an important decision needed to be made. Do we play this game tomorrow, or do we not? Death was not just a part of life, it was life. No matter how much you hated it or didn't want it to happen, it is one of those moments everyone must learn to live with and cope with. Once the guys had gathered themselves he informed the team about a call he made to Mike's parents before the meeting.

Gale and Joseph Albright knew most of the boys on the team. Mike was a senior, so over the past four years they had met many of the players. While speaking to Coach Castle they unquestionably wanted the kids to decide as a team if they should play the game tomorrow. They also expressed how they would stand behind whatever decision the team made. Before he hung up, Coach Castle asked Gale and Joseph if they would attend tomorrow's game if the kids decided to go forward and play. He said it would be in honor of Mike and the school would make sure he was remembered properly. They agreed and said there was no way Mike would want them to miss the game, even under these conditions.

After explaining all this to the team he asked them outright, "Guys, this one is up to you. You all decide and I will return in 15 minutes with the other coaches and get your answer." He also made it impeccably clear, whatever decision they made was fine by him, and they had the support of the school administrators as well.

Fifteen minutes later Coach Castle walked in the locker room and found his team hand in hand. When they saw him and the other coaches they raised their hands as one. Tears still in their eyes and never having said a word Coach Castle knew exactly what they were saying. He told them to do whatever they needed too and meet back in the locker room at 6pm. He said they would have a quick walk through practice as best as they could, talk about Vernon College, and bring this shitty day to a close.

When the practice was over and the guys had all gone, Coach Castle called the Albrights and told them the team had chosen to play the game. They cried and were proud of the kids. They knew this was tough on them as a family, but also knew the boys on that team loved Mike too. The fact they wanted to play seemed like a testament to the kind of young men Mike surrounded himself with. The Albright's confirmed they would be there for the kickoff and asked Coach Castle to bring Mike's home jersey to the field before the game so Gale could wear it. He agreed and they said their goodbye's for the night. After hanging up the phone Coach Castle sat and cried in his office. This was not just a playoff game, this was a game to honor a player he coached for the past four years, and a young man he also watched grow up. His assistant coaches continued preparing for tomorrow's game, but they didn't do it with dry eyes either.

About 180 miles away, Vernon College coach, Terry Mills, got a call from the administration of McKnight College informing him of the tragedy. Coach Mills responded with genuine sorrow and wished the school the best in trying to cope with such heartbreak. He was willing to agree to a postponement of the game if the NCAA approved, but McKnight College made it clear, the game will go on. He then called all of his coaches into a meeting and informed them of what happened. The room was quiet for a moment until offensive line coach Craig

Williams said he was going to say a prayer for the fallen player, his family, and his teammates. Every man in the room bowed their head and let the kind words soak in, they knew this could have easily been one of their own.

After the prayer Coach Mills called a local print shop and ordered round decals with the number #56 on them in Spartan's gold and red. After explaining the situation the local shop got right to work and delivered the decals a few hours later. The coaches took them and went through the Titans locker room placing a decal on the back of each player's helmet. Competition was a great thing, this was going to be a great game, but respect for a fellow player was the right thing to do.

As they were putting a decal on the last helmet they noticed it was only fifteen minutes before the guys would be coming in for practice. A light walk through and some game film study were planned, but the coaches knew there also had to be some personal time to reflect on what happened and what they would be experiencing tomorrow.

The first player to walk into the locker room was senior fullback and team captain, Troy Mertz. He saw the coaches and had been around long enough to know something was up. Coach Mills walked over and sat down with Troy at his locker. He showed him the decal they had placed on his helmet and began explaining the situation. Troy didn't know Mike, but he had studied defensive film of him for the past week. He had a lot of respect for the linebacker and was expecting a tough game between the tackles. As a player, Troy felt for Mike and his teammates.

As a person, he knew the parents must be devastated. He couldn't imagine the emotional strain he would experience while running out on that field had this been one of his guys. He also couldn't imagine what it would be like for his parents to attend the game if it were him taken too soon. The rush of emotions brought Troy to a decision. A decision he would share with his team shortly, one that he would make sure was carried out on a visitor's field if they won the game.

As the rest of the Titans made their way into the locker room, Troy informed them there would be a meeting before practice. One meeting with coach, then a quick meeting with him. Word spread fast and the players were in the meeting room seated waiting on the arrival of Coach Mills. In the meeting room players asked about the gold and red decal on their helmets, but no one knew what it was all about except Troy.

Coach Mills entered the meeting room with his staff and told the team about Mike Albright's untimely passing. He also explained that the kids from McKnight College made the decision to play the game tomorrow.

He had kind words for the fallen player, and kind words for the Spartan's team who made the choice to face adversity head on. "Gentlemen, those kids are just like you. They play this game with heart, determination, and pride. They take classes and are trying to make something of themselves. They deal with all the same issues as you do, but right now they are dealing with loss. Tomorrow they are our opponents, but they are also human beings and fellow football brothers. You go out there to win, but you show them respect as well. We placed decals on the back of your helmets in honor of Mike. Guys, this is real life. Things like this happen and could have easily happened to one of us. Word is his parents will be at the game, the stadium will be packed, and the emotions there will be overwhelming. We go play our game, we go there to win, but we go there and do so with class. I am proud of you guys and the season we have going this year. Make me proud tomorrow by not only winning, but showing the folks at McKnight we feel for their loss and our hearts go out to them."

The team sat silent, soaking in the reality of what happened and what was going to happen tomorrow. Young minds trying to comprehend death, life, winning, losing, pain, respect, etc… was easier for some than others, but they knew as a team they would follow their coaches' orders. Those thoughts were interrupted as Troy stood up and walked in front of his fellow teammates and coaches. Their team captain and senior leader had something to say and they knew it was time to pay attention.

Troy told his teammates about an idea he came up with if they won the game tomorrow. Explaining to them what he wanted to do and how it would happen had the guys shaking their heads in agreement. It had the coaches grinning from ear to ear to hear young men put others before themselves. Coach Mills listened to Troy's idea and admired such an act. He knew if they won and carried out his plan, it would be something special to see and something they could be proud of.

With all in agreement they started their walk through practice and refocused their minds on tomorrow's game. Two hours later they were finished and got their gear in check and packed for the long bus ride in the morning. Once everyone had all their ducks in a row they headed their separate ways for a bite to eat and to find a good night's sleep.

Back at McKnight College the student body held a candlelight vigil at the football field in Mike's honor. Banners were hung with his name and number around the stadium, the grounds keeping crew decided they would honor the young man by repainting the fifty yard line number. Normally the fifty yard line had a huge number 5 on one side of the line and a huge number 0 on the other. The crew painted over the zero so it matched the green grass and replaced it with a number 6. Having a 56 at midfield would entice emotion and motivate the Spartan's team. They had no idea if it was against NCAA regulations, but honestly didn't much care. Mike may not be there in body on Saturday, but with the wonderful outpouring of admiration for the young man by so many, he would be there in spirit.

Players from both schools were in their rooms getting ready for bed and coaches were finally closing up their offices and looking forward to some shut eye as well. It seemed like an eternity, but this tragic day was finally coming to an end.

GAMEDAY — DECEMBER 2ᴺᴰ, 2006

Loading up the bus, the Titans of Vernon College received a school spirited send off. A few hundred students and local fans were there to cheer on the boys as they prepared to head to McKnight. Well wishes, high fives, and plenty of hollering made the guys smile and helped them see this game was not just for them, it was for their school and their town. This is one of the main reasons why you play this great sport.

During the bus ride Troy played the game out in his mind a thousand times. Which plays would he lead block, which would he carry the ball. Did he stay in to block, or did he swing out into the flat as a safety valve for his quarterback? He also played out his intentions if they won. He knew getting a win was his main objective, but setting an example for his team to see was also an inspiring goal. Back and forth his mind went, from the playbook of the Titans offense to the reaction of those effected by Mike's death. Other players were listening to music with their own thoughts running through their minds. A three hour bus trip seemed to take forever, but when you kept your mind busy and prepared for battle, you were at your destination before you knew it.

Pulling up to the McKnight College campus, the emotions of today's game were evident. Banners for Mike Albright hung everywhere, while students and fans wearing gold and red were all over campus. The boys from Vernon College saw their colors mixed in, but they knew this was an away game. The home field advantage and twelfth man benefit belonged to the Spartan's.

The locker rooms were the same in so many aspects, but different just the same. The Titans were getting suited up, ankles were being taped, braces fitted just right, while players went over final preparations. Coaches were explaining different formations and calls that would be made under certain circumstances. The music was playing, the kids were pumped up and kept reminding themselves the National Championship game was within reach.

On the other side of the building, a Spartan's team was trying to accomplish the same tasks. Players were getting their pregame needs and coaches were giving them last minute instructions on what needed to be done once they took the field. The problem was emotions were a jumbled mess. Focusing was hard, but after a team meeting earlier in the morning over breakfast, it was made clear they had to push through all that for Mike. This game wasn't just a game anymore, it was a memorial in a sense. Their actions on this day could be talked about for years to come. They knew it, they felt it, now they just had to do it.

If there was any doubt in the teams mind about making the right call to play today's game, it was quickly whisked away when Coach Castle came into the locker room with Mike's parents in tow. He called the boys into the center of the room where they took a knee without ever being told too. The Albright's stood under the florescent lights with their heads high, but eyes bloodshot from tears. Mike's mother, Gale, wearing his home jersey, spoke first. She told the kids that she was proud of their decision to play the game today. She had no doubt in her mind Mike would have demanded they play. She knew what football meant to him, and she knew the game helped shape a young man's life and teach him valuable lessons. She wished them good luck and thanked them for the wonderful memories they made with her son. As she stepped back to let Mike's dad say a few words, the tears simply flowed. He saw the pain in their eyes and made sure they knew he supported their choice as well. Joseph then told them he and Gale would be on the sidelines watching the game.

He raised his voice like a father does to get his point across and told the Spartan's team, "My son loved this school, he loved this team, and he told me many times this team had all the pieces needed to win it all. If my son believed in you guys, then I believe in you guys. Don't you dare hang your heads, you hold them high and you take that field with pride. You play this game with heart and determination, and when it's over, if for some reason you're not the victors today, I will still be proud of every single one of you."

The Albright's thanked the coaches and team for allowing them to stop by and speak before the game. After they left to head to the field, the Spartan's team had a moment of silence for their fallen teammate and also for his family. They then stood and got ready to make their way to the field.

As the teams started leaving the locker rooms to line up in the small tunnels leading into the stadium, they both heard the McKnight band playing. Once they reached the end of their respective tunnels they could see a capacity crowd, they could see all of the material hung in remembrance of Mike, and they could see the beautiful fall day that awaited their performances. They remained in the tunnels as the band cleared the field and once they were out of the way, the announcer introduced the visiting Vernon College Titans. They blew out of the tunnel with thunder. Their royal blue and white uniforms matching the royal blue and white covering the visitor's side of the stadium. The applause were there, but muffled by boos from the McKnight faithful.

A few minutes later the stadium began to shake, and like an explosion of sound the home crowd unleashed their love for the McKnight College Spartan's as they took the field. Gold and red flags, foam fingers, and towels filled the air alongside the noise and band playing. This school and this crowd were excited about today and they showed it. The Spartan team gazed upon the number 56 painted at mid field, it was beyond touching.

After the captains came out for the coin toss and shook hands, McKnight won the toss and elected to receive. The National Anthem was played while everyone stood and respected the American tradition that occurs at all sporting events. When the anthem ended the announcer asked for a moment of silence and announced the death of starting linebacker and senior, Mike Albright. The stadium was silent and most in the crowd and on the field bowed their heads. The announcer broke the silence by informing the crowd Mike's parents were in attendance and standing on the Spartan's sideline. He told the crowd of roughly 9,000 Gale and Joseph's names, and identified them by their attire. Gale was wearing Mike's red home jersey with the number 56 in gold and his last name across the back in white. Mike's dad had on his trusty Spartan's hooded sweatshirt he had worn since Mike's freshman year. The entire crowd, both McKnight and Vernon fans, applauded the Albright's. The players on both sides of the field raised their helmets to the heavens while the Albright's looked on filled with grateful emotion.

After a few minutes the teams took the field and the semi-final playoff game was finally underway.

SPORTSMENSHIP AT ITS FINEST

With everything they had the Spartan's clawed, scratched, and fought like champions, but today wasn't going to be their day. Vernon College showed up to win, and win is what they were going to do. With 1:22 left in the game the Titans were winning 42-13 and their offense had just gotten the ball back on a fumble recovery. With the Spartan's having no more time outs, all Vernon College had to do was take a few kneel down snaps and they were on their way to playing Sunny Crest College of Texas for the Division III National Championship.

Surprisingly almost none of the Spartan fans left the game. Out of respect for Mike and his parent's being present they had stuck around to see this game through. A touching gesture that in mere moments would be rewarded with a display of sportsmanship no one knew was coming, except for the Titans.

It was 3rd and 10 with 0:27 seconds now remaining in the game when fullback Troy Mertz called a timeout. The crowd was confused, as was the Spartan team. Troy walked across the line of scrimmage and began to talk to McKnight senior defensive end, Jake Elder. All the crowd could see was the two young men talking and Jake shaking his head at Troy. The officials tried to step in, but with a few words from Troy, they backed off and let the guys talk during the timeout. With a pat on Jake's helmet, Troy walked back to the Titan huddle, while Jake huddled up the entire team and coaching staff of the Spartan's. As the timeout ran out and the referee's whistle blew, everyone was back in place except for the Titan's Troy Mertz who now lined up as the quarterback to take the final snap of the game. Confusion still obvious throughout the stadium, especially on the Vernon side where the Titan fans were elated, but had no idea what the team was doing.

Troy took the snap from center and quickly dropped to his knee, thus ending the game, but as quick as he knelt, he stood up and turned from the line of scrimmage and began walking towards Gale and Joseph Albright. With the game ball in hand and Mike's parents in sight, he could hear the Vernon fans cheering the monumental victory behind him. He could also hear the Vernon College band playing the school fight song, but in front of him were the parents of a young man who tragically lost his life just the day before. He could see the thousands of Spartan fans who remained in their seats watching him approach the family, wondering what he was doing. Joseph and Gale noticed he was walking towards them so they remained in place.

Troy walked up to Gale and Joseph Albright and introduced himself. Without saying another word, he dropped to one knee in front of them and bowed his head. Everyone was so busy trying to process what he was doing, only a few immediately noticed that both teams had approached the Albright's and were now right behind Troy. Within seconds, the crowd watched as every player from both teams took a knee, and bowed their heads towards Mike's parents. A sea of gold, blue, red, and white now appeared as one. Each player placing one of their hands on another's shoulder pads, regardless of what jersey he wore.

Tears began to stream down the faces of the Albright's, down the faces of the Spartan players and their fans. The Vernon College faithful realized their boys were paying respects to Mike's parents and to McKnight College. No one moved. Those who were walking out of the stadium stopped and turned back to see this display of sportsmanship. For almost a full two minutes the only sound heard among 9,000 people was a few sniffles and weeps from the emotional yet incredible atmosphere.

As private prayers and the moment of silence ended Troy stood giving Gale a hug and shaking Joseph's hand. Everyone continued to watch as the game ball was then handed to Joseph. With this gesture the Spartan crowd began to clap. Vernon's fan base also began to applaud. In mere moments the 9,000 people in attendance were responding with appreciation of this kind act.

Coach Castle approached Troy and handed him his headset. During the timeout Troy had asked Jake to find out if their coach's headset could be used as a microphone over the stadiums sound system. If it could, he asked to be given the headset after presenting the game ball to Mike's parents. Well, with headset in hand, Troy's question had been answered.

He put the headset on and said, "TEST, TEST, is this working?" The fans let him know it was and he could also hear himself through the speakers.

"My name is Troy Mertz, I'm a senior at Vernon College. Today is the biggest win of my career, and in our school's history. I am thankful for that and will celebrate it, but not here. Yesterday we learned of Mike's death. I cannot in good conscious celebrate on his field or in his stadium. We will have plenty of time for that back home. Instead our team has decided to honor Mike and his parents the best way we can. Today's game ball has been given to Gale and Joseph Albright. A little research before today told me Mike never missed a game in his four years here. I watched him this week on film and he was one hell of a football player. This being the only game he ever missed in a Spartan uniform leaves no doubt he is today's most valuable player. I cannot imagine what you all are feeling, but please know this team and Vernon College share in your grief. Mike was a brother on the gridiron and that deserves our respect."

Troy continued as everyone in the stadium listened to him attentively. "Mr. and Mrs. Albright, I hope you take this game ball as not only a reminder of today where your son lived on through his team, his school, and these fans, but as a token of respect from us. We all wish we could have banged heads with your son today. I don't know if the outcome would have been different, but sharing the field with him would have been an honor."

A look around the stadium and it was evident this event and Troy's words were not going unnoticed. Tears filled the stands, applause again filled the air, but Gale's movement with her hands towards the headset told Troy she too wanted to say a few words.

As he took it off and handed it to her, the crowd noise intensified and everyone there wanted her to know she and her husband were in their thoughts and they wanted to hear what she was about to say. With the headset on she waited a few moments for the applause to die down, then softly thanked everyone for their compassion. As the crowd quieted, Gale said, "Thank you all so much for the banners, the 56 at midfield, and the outpouring of support for Mike. Today wasn't easy, and neither will the next few days, weeks, or years. My son loved this school and his teammates and this just solidifies why."

After gathering herself, she continued, "Troy and to all the Titans, thank you so much for this. I cannot put into words what your prayers and display of respect for my son mean to us. We will forever keep this game ball and forever remember this day. You young men should be proud of yourselves. Not just for winning this game, but for having this kind of thoughtfulness. It's moments like this people never forget and thanks to you, today will be a memory etched in the minds of those fortunate enough to have seen it. Thank you guys and thank you Vernon College, we will not forget this."

The stadium flared up as Troy and Gale hugged one last time. As their embrace separated one of the Spartan players raised his helmet skyward, followed by a few more, followed by every player on the field. This was their goodbye as the season for the Spartans was officially over. The Titans shook hands and hugged the Spartan players. Wishing them the best and getting the same in return. Many of the Spartan's players telling the Titans to go bring that National Championship home to Pennsylvania. They made it clear, if anyone deserved it, the Vernon College boys did.

As the Titan's walked off the field they were met with applause, good lucks and many thanks from the Spartan fans. Today was obviously more than just about football, but football is what brought this all together and everyone there knew it.

RETURNING THE FAVOR

Back home the Vernon College Titans celebrated and celebrated big time. School spirit was an understatement. Banners, paintings, flags, etc... were everywhere on campus. The local news and newspapers ran the story about the team's display of sportsmanship, but also ran stories about their victory and upcoming Championship game against the Sunny Crest Panthers.

There wasn't much need for the locals to write a story about what Troy and the Titans did for the Albrights, a few uploaded videos of their actions on YouTube took care of that. Nationwide, people watched and commented on the event. Millions of people expressed how proud they were of the Titans and how awesome it was to see the videos. Major networks took note and ran the full story. Within 48 hours of getting back home the Titans were the talk of the college football world and the National Championship game was getting more attention than usual.

Coach Mills let the boys enjoy their moment, they deserved it, but then had to reign them back in and start preparations for the Panthers. The Titans were about to travel to Virginia and play for a DIII National Title on a national stage.

After a week of good practices, film study, and preparation, the Titans were as ready as they could be. The school was too. They chartered buses to the game for all students who wanted to go, and local business's chipped in to get buses for any fans who wanted to make the trip.

The local bars and pubs advertised when they would be airing the game on the big screens, with food and drinks available. The school also made the auditorium accessible for those who wanted to see the game, but couldn't travel. This would be the big event before Christmas break and students were ready to contribute before heading home.

The Titans were again sent off in grand fashion as their bus pulled away from campus and headed towards Virginia two days before the game. Students lined campus streets, local fans lined the town streets, and both wore their Titan apparel, waved their Titan flags, and cheered letting the guys know they were behind them. Troy took it all in, loving every moment, as did every member of the team. Now it was time to relax as a nine hour bus trip was underway.

As the Titans bus rolled down Interstate 95, something unexpected was happening in their honor. Back at McKnight College, the Spartan's football team decided they needed to thank the boys from Vernon for what they had done for Mike and his family. Jake Elder, the senior defensive end Troy talked too on the field to set his plan in motion the week prior, went to Coach Castle who in turn went to the school administrators about the team's proposal.

Jake and the guys were asking that McKnight College bus them, and any other students or local folks who wished to go watch the Titans, to Virginia. He knew, unfortunately, that there would be plenty of seats available in the stadium that was selected to host the game. According to news sources Vernon College expected approximately 1,500 fans to show up in Virginia and Sunny Crest estimated around 1,000 to be in attendance. With local Virginian's coming out just to see a game in their back yard, Jake figured attendance totals to be around three to six thousand in a stadium built for 10,000. He wanted the guys from Vernon to feel as supported as possible.

The school administrators didn't waste a moment. They agreed to charter buses to take the entire Spartan football team and coaches, along with enough buses to transport 1,000 students or fans who wished to go along. They did leave the task of filling those buses up to Jake and the football team. A challenge they willingly accepted and got started on within minutes of being given the go ahead.

Jake called the Albright's who, without hesitation, accepted and said they would be glad to go. As football players ran around town and around campus, they were filling up the buses quicker than they anticipated. People wanted to be a part of something special, and this would be special.

By the following morning the Spartan football team had a list of 1,000 names and their contact information who were willing and wanted to travel to Virginia to watch the game. In their brief to each person they spoke too, they made it clear Spartan apparel was to be worn to the game. They wanted the Titans to know they were there as proud Spartans, but really there to thank and support the Titans for their act of graciousness.

It was now game day in Roanoke, Virginia and the Titans were getting themselves ready for the last game of the year. Troy and the other seniors knew this was their final game, but in their minds how could the last time wearing the blue and white be any better.

ESPN had their cameras in position, the film truck and satellite dishes were in place, people were coming in the stadium getting their seats and the 2006 Division III National Championship was about thirty minutes away from kickoff.

The stadium looked like most you'll find in college football, well almost. The home side was filled with the royal blue and white of the Vernon Titans, while the green and black of Sunny Crest was shone across the way. The thing that caught everyone's eye was the large amount of gold and red filling up the north end zone seating area. Vernon fans figured it out quickly and were grateful for the support shown by a school and team that had just suffered through a tragedy. The Sunny Crest fans also figured it out and understood what they were doing.

ESPN announcers noticed this as well, and as the live broadcast kicked off they mentioned how McKnight College fans came today in support of the Titans. The nation by now was aware of what occurred a week ago and how Vernon College put the loss of the Spartan's linebacker before themselves, and that act deserved a different kind of thank you.

With the Panthers already on the field, Vernon College stood in the tunnel and Troy noticed the gold and red section in the end zone. He then noticed two familiar faces standing between the tunnel and the field. Mr. and Mrs. Albright stood there looking at the team who treated their son with such dignity and respect. Mom wearing Mike's home jersey and Dad in the trusty old Spartan's hoody, Troy noticed they added a Titan's towel to todays colors. When their eyes and Troy's met just before the team ran onto the field, Joseph twirled that flag above his head and Gale clapped with a smile. Troy's eyes glazed over, but his excitement of running onto that field kept him in check.

When the Titan's team saw the gold and red of McKnight College in the end zone, they ran as one to the barrier about ten feet from the stands. The Spartan's stood and pointed at the Titans, the Titans returned the sentiment by raising their helmets to the sky. The respect shown by the Titans a week before, was now being reciprocated and no words could describe what it meant to the boys of Vernon.

A little over three hours later the scoreboard reflected the outcome. The winning fans and team remained on the field waiting for the National Championship Trophy presentation, while those who lost received their second place plaque and gave the stage to the triumphant. This was their moment, for all the nation to see.

You might ask, well who won, but this story isn't about winners and losers, it's about dreams, life, compassion, sportsmanship, and respect. At the end of the day, whether you win them all, or lose them all, life goes on and its realities remain to test your resolve. Football has always been and will continue to be a great escape. A wonderful time for people to come together and forget the horrors of the real world. To put on hold stressful events, to take a break before getting back to the daily grind.

On that note though, the sky sure was a pretty blue that day, the clouds were fluffy white, and it was exactly 56 degrees the entire game. The rest as they say, is history.

Zechariah 10:5